THIS JOURNAL BELONGS TO

INTRODUCTION

Creativity is our lifeblood. Though it is inseparable from us, we may forget it's even there. It's easy to convince ourselves that we're not creative. We tell ourselves stories about our lack of talent and why we decided to get a 'real' job. There are myriad reasons, stories, and convincing voices that inhibit us from living a joyfully creative life or from even letting ourselves doodle on a napkin.

I don't presume to know your unique relationship with art, but I do assure you that you are not alone in your fears and inhibitions. And, I know that creative permission is one of the most generous gifts you could ever give yourself. One of my greatest missions is to help rekindle the spark of curiosity within others, to stoke the fire of vision, and to fan the flames of artistic empowerment.

The creative process can be approached from countless directions, as unique as you and the facet of your individual perspective. There is no wrong way to make art, no rules, no limits. Only you know what makes your spirit sing, and only you can claim it for yourself. Though we may look to others for inspiration, guidance, tools, and techniques, the creative path is a solitary one. It is fortified by brave expression, faith in the process, and a willingness to show up and take risks. These practices are cultivated, not inherent. Depending on our history and trauma around art-making, it may take more effort for some to allow this unfettered flow of creativity. When we dance to the tune of inspiration, we must let it lead. We can train our steps and get to know the rhythm, but we must also surrender to the guidance of the divine creative spirit that is coursing through us. We must be willing or even eager to make mistakes, to step into the unknown, and be swept away by the mystery.

There is no safety net in the creative process, and to be honest, you don't need one. Though it can at times feel like a monumental undertaking, it is also helpful to remember how silly and trivial it all is. Paint is simply colourful mud smeared on a piece of fabric. Dance is the erratic flailing of limbs in the air. We are each just a tiny speck, on a tiny speck, hurtling through space. It's really not that big a deal. So, we can all just relax, take a breath, make a colourful mess, and let ourselves have fun.

I believe all of this to be true, along with the potent paradox of creativity. Art is meaningless and at the same time, profoundly important. The world depends on each of our enlivened hearts and inspired art. Creative expression can heal emotional trauma, cure illness, and fill the body, heart, and mind with renewed vitality and joy. Each creation also has the potential to move mountains, individually and culturally. It can awaken and empower the viewer and connect straight to the subconscious. It can speak truth and shine light on critical issues. It can start revolutions, shift paradigms, and offer mirrors and templates of grand potential and solutions, paths forward towards healing and wholeness.

So, make art, no matter how well or beautiful. Create as if your life and the world depend on it. And yet, don't take it too seriously. Laugh at the petty judgments, dance with the lofty expectations, play and make a mess, retain a beginner's mind, and know that you are divinely supported in your unique expression. The worst that can happen is that you muck up a piece of paper, one that will never again be pristine white and will now and forever be marred by your scribbles. The most that can happen is that you come alive. The creative spark in you will be stoked with every line and dot until an inspired fire rages in you so brightly that it ignites others around you. At the very least, you will liberate yourself from an artless reality, and at the most, you will help save the world.

Thank you for sharing your unique expression.

With love,

Where the spirit does not work with the hand, there is no art.
— Leonardo da Vinci

The fairest thing we can experience is the mysterious. It is the fundamental emotion which stands at the cradle of true art and true science.

— Albert Einstein

Creativity takes courage.
— Henri Matisse

Art enables us to find ourselves and lose ourselves at the same time.
— Thomas Merton

A picture is a poem without words.

— Horace

Creativity is allowing yourself to make mistakes.
Art is knowing which ones to keep.
— Scott Adams

Every artist dips his brush in his own soul, and paints his own nature into his pictures.
— Henry Ward Beecher

The essence of all beautiful art, all great art, is gratitude.
— Friedrich Nietzsche

It is truly brave to trust the wild inclinations of a creative heart.
And it is the only option.

Human salvation lies in the hands of the creatively maladjusted.
— Martin Luther King Jr

In honour of the Ancestors. May they guide and teach us. May they forgive our mistakes, and may their mistakes be made right by our healing.

In honour of the strength of each Generation. May the profound wisdom we each carry be a light that brings deepened understanding and grace to our individual path.

In honour of all aspects of our Self: our inner Maiden, Mother, Crone. May they live in balance within each of us.

In honour of the lifetimes that we have each walked before, the lifetimes that will echo on into our Soul's continued journey. May we continue to grow and evolve. May we always seek light, and be light.

In honour of the Past, the Present, and the Future. May we breathe into each moment, knowing there is only Now.

Imagination is more important than knowledge.

— Albert Einstein

Beauty will save the world.

— Dostoevsky

Sometimes the questions are complicated and the answers are simple.

— Dr. Seuss

To be an artist is to believe in life.

— Henry Moore

Inspiration does exist, but it has to find you working.

— Pablo Picasso

A true artist is not one who is inspired but one who inspires others.
— Salvador Dalí

My role in society, or any artist's or poet's role,
is to try and express what we all feel. Not to tell people how to feel.
Not as a preacher, not as a leader, but as a reflection of us all.

— John Lennon

Art is a relentless teacher.

It shows me again and again the deep lessons of patience and humility. It challenges me to trust the process, be present, and exercise the diligent dedication that creative practice demands.

Art is a persistent teacher.

It reminds me that creativity is a journey, not a destination. It takes incredible willpower to know that there are hundreds of hours of work remaining, and yet sit down at the easel and continue on, one brushstroke at a time. It is my joyful meditation; otherwise, I could go mad from tedium.

Art is a humbling teacher.

This is not glamorous work. It is innumerable hours spent in isolation, back strained and eyes focused, caressing worlds out of nothingness. It demands my unwavering trust, my complete attention, and my deep surrender. It requires me to dedicate my body, mind, spirit, resources, and time, and to unapologetically bare it to the world, my soul naked for all to see and judge. I cannot be discouraged by criticism, nor can I rely on approval.

Art is a profound teacher.

It continues to show me new depths of how to walk gracefully in the world: to be present with the process, get out of the way, to choose where I put my attention, and to do my best with the tools and skill I have. It grants me the faith that every detail, no matter how trivial or unplanned, is part of an elaborate whole, and that someday I'll look back and it will all make sense.

Art is a loving teacher.

When I trust the process and honour it with my attention and intention, it takes me to places I could never dream. It is my benevolent guide for the boundless potential of imagination, it is my muse who whispers me awake in the morning, and my friend who rewards my loyalty with unfathomable blessings.

The creative union of the conscious with the unconscious is what one usually calls 'inspiration.'

— Leon Trotsky

It's not what you look at that matters, it's what you see.
— Henry David Thoreau

The creative process is a process of surrender, not control.

— Julia Cameron

I would like to paint the way a bird sings.

— Claude Monet

The sovereign state of my purest source,
cannot be swayed by an outer force.
Built upon my deepest being,
truest knowing, and boundless seeing.
Only in this place of wholeness,
can I mirror another's fullness.
And not without our selfless giving,
can we unite in blissful living.

The more I think it over, the more I feel that there is nothing more truly artistic than to love people.

— Vincent van Gogh

Artists serve as mediums between the mundane and the divine.

— Inga Musico

Creativity is sacred, and it is not sacred. What we make matters enormously, and it doesn't matter at all. We toil alone, and we are accompanied by spirits. We are terrified, and we are brave. Art is a crushing chore and a wonderful privilege. Only when we are at our most playful can divinity finally get serious with us. Make space for all these paradoxes to be equally true inside your soul, and I promise—you can make anything.

— Elizabeth Gilbert

All true artists, whether they know it or not, create from a place of no-mind,
from inner stillness.

— Eckhart Tolle

I offer a reminder that you are divine. This life is an opportunity to explore and grow; this body, a vessel to nurture and enjoy; this moment, a responsibility to create, to celebrate, to share, and to remind others that they too are divine.

*Creativity is a lot like happiness. It shows up when
you're thinking of something else.*

— Bert Dodson

All I did was to look at what the universe showed me,
to let my brush bear witness to it.

— Claude Monet

I'm not telling you it's going to be easy – I'm telling you it's going to be worth it.
— Art Williams

You can't be content with mastery; you have to push yourself
to become a student again.

— Austin Kleon

You need the dark in order to show the light.
— Bob Ross

In the beginning God created the heavens and the earth.

— Genesis 1:1

Practicing an art, no matter how well or badly, is a way to make your soul grow,
for heaven's sake. Sing in the shower. Dance to the radio. Tell stories. Write a poem
to a friend, even a lousy poem. Do it as well as you possibly can. You will get an
enormous reward. You will have created something.

— Kurt Vonnegu

Step onto the road and there's no telling where you might be swept off to.

— JRR Tolkien

We need not close our eyes to the pains of the world, for they cannot be healed if we chose to ignore them. Instead, we witness, eyes and hearts open, and through acceptance and compassion, we travelled transmute the shadow into light, the fear into love.

In honour of the sacred and life-giving water that flows through us, and all things. This water is more ancient than the earth itself, and will never cease to be. The same drops that once fell in an Indian Monsoon, another time flowed down the Amazon and then was sipped in a fine cup of tea in China. It floated in mists over the Orkney Isles, was distilled into tinctures by medicine makers, and crashed in thunderous waves against the shores of Hawaii. It moistened a tissue to wipe a child's face, dripped from cedar branches onto mossy forest floors, swirled in snowstorms on the mountaintops of the Alps, and was mixed with pigments to paint masterpieces throughout the ages. It is the same water that flows from our eyes in a moment of pure emotion. Like the spark of our spirit, water is eternal, only changing shape and expression as it journeys through existence in a timeless dance.

May you have song in every breath, dance in every step, and prayer in every heartbeat.

Decide what is sacred to you, and put your best life energies at its service.
Make that the focus of your studies, your work, the test for your pleasures and
your relationships. Don't ever let fear or craving for security turn you aside.

— Starhawk

The visual language is a lost language, like cyphers undecyphered. But it underlies all that we dream each night. It invisibly appears whenever the images of vision flow in a meaningful way. It emerges from trance, contemplation, myth and madness. This ancient image-language, otherwise forgotten, is now being spoken once more.

— Laurence Caruana

Sometimes you will never know the value of a moment,
until it becomes a memory.

— Dr. Seuss

Throw your heart into the picture and then jump in after it.

— Howard Pyle

If you're alive, you're a creative person.
— Elizabeth Gilbert

As you move toward a dream, the dream moves toward you.

— Julia Cameron

The aim of art is to represent not the outward appearance of things,
but their inward significance.

— Aristotle

Art should comfort the disturbed and disturb the comfortable.

— Banksy

I paint in a dance between divine grace and conscious attention.
I strive to "get out of the way" to allow spirit to speak through me,
all the while staying present and diligent to the task at hand.
With every brushstroke, I witness worlds unfold before me.
Each canvas takes me on a journey, and as my paintbrush follows,
I am led back to my centre.

Colour is a power which directly influences the soul.
— Wassily Kandinsky

I honour you for your unique expression, your creative hands, your boundless compassion, and your unwavering bravery to share yourself with the world. In each moment that we choose love and connection over fear and separation, we are healing our ancestors, the generations to come, and the earth on which we live. Though our stories may be spoken in unfamiliar languages, and we may wear strange adornments and address God by another name, we are all woven together. We are threads in the same tapestry, sovereign yet supported, and made stronger and brighter by each other. This is a co-creation, a grand masterpiece. So keep faith, beloved friends. Choose love, and together let's continue this Light Work.

Let all that you do be done in love.

— 1 Corinthians 16:14

Art is a collaboration between God and the artist,
and the less the artist does the better.

— Andre Gide

Art can never be understood but can only be seen as a kind of magic,
the most profound and mysterious of human activities.
— Bill Reid

The artist's task is to save the soul of humanity. If the artists cannot find the way,
then the way cannot be found.

— Terence McKenna

I will not follow where the path may lead, but I will go where there is no path,
and I will leave a trail.

— Muriel Strode

Life is a balance between holding on and letting go.

— Rumi

Inside you there's an artist you don't know about.

— Rumi

The role of the artist is especially crucial at this challenging and exciting time, while the world is at the precipice of momentous change. We have an opportunity to transmute the shadow and pain that we witness in the world around us into visions of wholeness. Artists are mapmakers, and those maps can help guide humanity forward into new and positive ways of seeing and being.

Never explain, never retract, never apologize,
just get the thing done and let them howl.
— Nellie McClung

Our deepest fear is not that we are inadequate. Our deepest fear is that we are powerful beyond measure. It is our light, not our darkness, that most frightens us. Your playing small does not serve the world. There is nothing enlightened about shrinking so that other people won't feel insecure around you. We are all meant to shine as children do. It's not just in some of us; it is in everyone. And as we let our own lights shine, we unconsciously give other people permission to do the same. As we are liberated from our own fear, our presence automatically liberates others.

— Marianne Williamson

If you feel safe in the area you're working in, you're not working in the right area. Always go a little further into the water than you feel you're capable of being in. Go a little bit out of your depth. And when you don't feel that your feet are quite touching the bottom, you're just about in the right place to do something exciting.

— David Bowie

Nothing is more important than reconnecting with your bliss.
Nothing is as rich. Nothing is more real.

— Deepak Chopra

*Nature, in her raw and untameable essence, will never be fully
bridled and held. This is the dance of existence, a desperate
longing of union and balance, the push and pull of chaos and
order. It is the dance of the masculine and feminine within us all.*

*Don't ask yourself what the world needs. Ask yourself what makes you come alive,
and go do that, because what the world needs is people who have come alive.*

— Howard Thurman

There are a thousand ways to kneel and kiss the earth.

— Rumi

We must be willing to let go of the life we planned so as
to have the life that is waiting for us.

— Joseph Campbell

Let yourself be silently drawn by the strange pull of what you really love.
It will not lead you astray.

— Rumi

I feel a deep stirring, a potent blossoming of creativity. It is all around us, gaining momentum in our own lives, in those of our family and community, and the collective experience. I believe it is our divine responsibility to create and to share inspiration, especially at this time of change. As we honour our personal creative paths, we contribute vitally to the whole through our own well-being, and by inspiring those around us to create as well.

We don't make mistakes, just happy little accidents.

— Bob Ross

The principles of true art is not to portray, but to evoke.

— Jerzy Kosinski

Creativity is contagious, pass it on.
— Albert Einstein

If you hear a voice within you saying, "You are not a painter," then by all means paint, and that voice will be silenced, but only by working.

— Vincent van Gogh

To draw you must close your eyes and sing.

— Pablo Picasso

Painting is self-discovery. Every good artist paints what he is.
— Jackson Pollock

The storm of our mind, our life, or the world around us can be tumultuous. At times it is truly terrifying, coming in mighty waves of intensity and gusts of raw force. It may bring up fears, old traumas, or trigger our fight or flight and survival instincts. It shakes us to our foundation, rattling the windows of our heart, tempting us to let the chaos in and to succumb to the fury of these troubled times. But, if we can remember our centre, our infinite spirit, we can remain steady and calm. We are witness to the madness and the confusion, and still, we hold our inner peace. Our compassionate heart becomes a beacon of light in the raging storm so that others might also find the True Harbor of their innermost stillness.

True North is the internal guide that navigates us through life. It is our constant and steady bearing, the fixed point in a turbulent world. It is always available to us when we can calm our mind and reconnect to our intuition. It is the compass of the heart.

Painting is poetry that is seen rather than felt,
and poetry is painting that is felt rather than seen.
— Leonardo da Vinci

The artist is a receptacle for emotions that come from all over the place:
from the sky, from the earth, from a scrap of paper, from a passing shape,
from a spider's web.

— Pablo Picasso

As in any form of creativity, when we are able to release judgment, move past our mind, breathe deep into the process, and find bliss in each step, we realize we are boundlessly assisted in our authentic and heart-centred expression. We are able to see that the art is not born of us, but through us, and in this knowing, we are humbled yet profoundly empowered. The more profound our art, the less we can take credit for it.

Art should be something that liberates your soul,
provokes the imagination and encourages people to go further.
— Keith Haring

He discovered his genius the day he dared to stop pleasing.
— Andre Malraux, on Goya

I am always doing that which I can not do; in order that I may learn how to do it.

— Pablo Picasso

The essential thing is to work in a state of mind that approaches prayer.

— Henri Matisse

You see things; and you say, 'Why?' But I dream things that never were;
and I say, 'Why not'?
— George Bernard Shaw

Anyhow, the older I get, the less impressed I become with originality. These days, I'm far more moved by authenticity. Attempts at originality can often feel forced and precious, but authenticity has quiet resonance that never fails to stir me.
— Elizabeth Gilbert

It's a simple and generous rule of life that whatever you practice, you will improve at.
— Elizabeth Gilbert

Every child is an artist until he's told he's not an artist.

— John Lennon

_____

_____

_____

_____

_____

_____

_____

_____

_____

_____

I don't believe in artist blocks. I do believe that we can be scared of the creative process, bored of our routine work, or put ourselves under too much pressure in our art-making. Creativity is not a well that can run dry, but it can be muddied by expectations, habits, and fears. If you feel the sticky inertia of stasis and your creativity seems stifled or silenced, it may be time to take a risk. This is a time to be brave, to take a leap of faith, to try something new and make a mess. It's okay to be afraid, but do not let that fear paralyze you. Grab some cardboard and scribble on it with a piece of charcoal or a chunk of red beet. Go to the beach and draw in the sand, knowing that the tide will come and wash it clean again. Do something silly, messy, and different — something that gets your whole body involved so you can get out of your head. Don't try to make something precious, beautiful, important, or marketable. Become a child again, uninhibited by the pressures of society and the weighty ideas of good versus bad art. Be innocent in your creative exploration, even just for a few moments. When you arrive back to the studio — with colour under your fingernails, sand between your toes, and adventure in your eyes — you will have gained fresh perspective, and I guarantee that the block which appeared so monumental before, is now less than a pebble. You've tricked it and taken a detour, and surely found new treasures along the way.

We are all searching for home — the land from which our bones were born. We long for belonging, to know a place deep in our feet and fingertips, to feel our heartbeat and tears as one with the stones and rivers.

We are orphans, you see, displaced cultures and spirit. Our lineage lost, abandoned, stolen, hidden. Along the way, we forgot the path home. We had to. It was a matter of survival. We had to begin anew, carve a hopeful future and liberate our stories from the weight of the past. Our allegories and songs faded from our lips; our rituals and customs became buried under layers of shame and fear; our heirlooms burned. We do not even recognize our reflection in the lakes anymore. We no longer hear our grandmother's voice in the wind.

How can we feel at home when we've forgotten what home feels like?

Perhaps if we just stop running for a moment, take off our shoes and dig our toes into the dirt, we might begin to remember. If we can pause and take a deep breath, feel the sun on our face and wind in our hair, we might hear the distant echoing of familiar songs and laughter. If we quiet our striving and lay our body on the land, we might notice our heartbeat slow and sync with the rhythm of the earth, and the blood in our veins weave in tune with the flowing water beneath the ground.

For what has been forgotten is not really gone. Though we have travelled far, we have not actually left.

The more miles I walk, the more I realize that home is under my feet and always has been. My roots remain tethered and true. I belong here, wherever I might place each next footstep. If I pay attention, I can notice the earth rise subtly up to meet my touch, welcoming me home. And, in turn, I can offer gratitude, and allow myself to sink a little deeper into her embrace.

"Thank you, Grandmother. I love you. Please forgive my forgetfulness. I remember now. With you I belong."

Have no fear of perfection, you'll never reach it.
— Salvador Dalí

Curiosity about life in all of its aspects, I think,
is still the secret of great creative people.
— Leo Burnett

You can't wait for inspiration, you have to go after it with a club.

— Jack London

Think left and think right and think low and think high.
Oh, the thinks you can think up if only you try.

— Dr. Seuss

Creativity is more than just being different. Anybody can plan weird; that's easy. What's hard is to be as simple as Bach. Making the simple, awesomely simple, that's creativity.

— Charles Mingus

Don't think. Thinking is the enemy of creativity. It's self-conscious, and anything self-conscious is lousy. You can't try to do things. You simply must do things.

— Ray Bradbury

An artist should never be a prisoner of himself, prisoner of style, prisoner of reputation, prisoner of success.

— Henri Matisse

*The world always seems brighter when you've just made something
that wasn't there before.*

— Neil Gaiman

I have been searching for inspiration and finding it in every luminous moment.
I have been wandering throughout mindscapes and landscapes.
I have been opening my hands to give, opening my arms to embrace, opening
my mind to awaken, opening my heart to love. I am on a tireless journey to the
highest potential of my spirit.

The best reason to paint is that there is no reason to paint.

— Keith Haring

Equinox: At this time of balanced day and night, the duality between light and dark becomes heightened and tangible, and with it comes the opportunity of reflection and spiritual transformation. In the cycle of birth, life, and death, we are reminded that often things must die before they can become reborn. The flower must wither and fade before it can release its seeds, the salmon must return to freshwater, the place of her birth, and surrender her life in order to release her eggs. We must breathe in and out to survive, a balance of yin and yang, giving and receiving. Spiritual ascent first requires descent, and through the willingness to go deep within ourselves we face own inner darkness, shining the light of understanding and acceptance. This is the alchemy of transformation, turning our shadow into pure gold.

Reclaim the sacredness of this life, the potency and magic of it and your place within this time and space. Celebrate the unique facet of your perspective, the temple of your body that is home to your indwelling spirit, that which is also connected and one with the Divine. Breathe, quiet your mind and be still; or dance, laugh, and howl at the moon. Whatever you do, do it with gratitude.

Art, it is said, is not a mirror, but a hammer: it does not reflect, it shapes.

— Leon Trotsky

Only when he no longer knows what he is doing does the painter do good things.

— Edgar Degas

I like nonsense, it wakes up the brain cells.

— Dr. Seuss

Art is the concrete representation of our most subtle feelings.
— Agnes Martin

Be the weirdo who dares to enjoy.

— Elizabeth Gilbert

Choose only one master – Nature.

— Rembrandt

Knowing how to look is a means of inventing.

— Salvador Dalí

*I offer each of my paintings as a mirror, a reminder of our pure
and good human heart, as well as our timeless divine spirit.*

It's better to create something that others criticise
than to create nothing and criticise others.
— Ricky Gervais

I just wanna make the world a better looking place.
If you don't like it, you can paint over it!
— Banksy

I'm not performing miracles, I'm using up and wasting a lot of paint.
— Claude Monet

The white stag appears in numerous mythologies around the world. In legends of King Arthur, the uncatchable White Hart represents humanity's spiritual quest, always something just out of reach. In Christian symbolism, the white stag is sometimes seen as a symbol of Jesus. Japan was said to be discovered when two brothers were in pursuit of the enchanting creature. The Celts believe that the White Stag was an agent from the Other World and a bringer of great change to those it encountered, and it often appeared when some sacred law was being broken.

This painting, Perseverance, speaks to the mighty spirit and pure heart of the Forest. In its shortsightedness, humanity may have tainted the wild, but Life will prevail, and the balance will be restored. The White Hart beckons us forward on our journey of awakening and awareness, calling us to step up bravely for the healing and wholeness of the entire interconnected Web of Life.

I am curious. I'm diving in and exploring, inquiring into myself and my inner workings. I'm watching my actions, my reactions, my assumptions, my beliefs. I'm igniting the torch of awareness and shining it in the dark corners of my unconscious. It's humbling work. It's sticky work. It's potent and exciting work. I am vigilant. I am brave. I am willing to be wrong, and I give myself permission to change my opinion and attend to each moment with a beginner's mind. I am willing to be misunderstood, and I give myself permission to speak my truth regardless. I realize that my truth is not a fixed point — it ebbs and flows with the tides of my heart. I will continue to do my best to be patient with others as they too shift. My relationship with myself and the world is a living organism, and it is growing and changing, adapting and refining. I am softening, and I am growing more fierce. I am detaching from what I thought it would look like. I am aligning with the mystery. I am stepping into authority in my own life, calling in what I desire and need, letting go of what no longer serves my highest good. I am shedding layers of preconceptions and prejudices. I am drawing healthy boundaries and cloaking myself in compassion, showing up more vulnerable and present than I was capable of when I only aimed to please. I am savouring the process of deepening and expansion. I am enough, even in my imperfection, in my quietude and in my wildness. I am curious. I am learning to live and living to learn.

If I could say it in words there would be no reason to paint.

— Edward Hopper

We must do our work for its own sake, not for fortune or attention or applause.

— Steven Pressfield

Great art transcends its culture and touches on that which is eternal.
— Madeleine L'Engle

Art is the only way to run away without leaving home.

— Twyla Tharp

They say everything looks better with odd numbers of things.
But sometimes I put even numbers – just to upset the critics.

— Bob Ross

I have always felt that I am divinely assisted in my art. The assistance is not tangible or nameable, but I often feel it there, like benevolent electricity in the air. Inspirations and ideas come into my mind at the perfect moments, urging me onward, and sometimes guiding me in directions that even I don't understand at the time. When I trust that I am supported — my spirit guiding my heart, my heart guiding my paintbrush — the destination is always far more magical than I could have consciously planned.

You cannot be all things to all people. Be unique. Be different. Give to others what you want yourself. And do what you were made to do.

— Robert Kiyosaki

To this day, no one has come up with a set of rules for originality. There aren't any.

— Les Paul

Unlock those places in you that long to soar. Be brave, dear heart, open and let go. Allow your spirit to be stirred by the rustle of feathers and the beating of wings. Let the wind lift you, and the boundless skies embrace you. You are safe. You are free. Live with wild abandon.

In the darkness of the earth, a seed dares to crack open. Against all the odds, without logic, and in a struggle against gravity, that seed sends a tender sprout out and up. With persistence it bursts through the surface of the soil, and the warm sun greets the sprout's newness with eager and unconditional adoration. Fortifying in strength and stature, it grows and stands taller, and eventually it becomes brave enough to form a bud. This bud is tiny and shy at first, but with the earth's stability and the sun's encouragement, the bud slowly unfurls its gifts, petal by petal. When we are brave and share our gifts and encourage others to do the same, together we are a garden.

If you ever find that you're the most talented person in the room,
you need to find another room.

— Austin Kleon

All artists are willing to suffer for their work.
But why are so few prepared to learn to draw?

— Banksy

*The seed of your next artwork lies embedded in the imperfections
of your current piece.*

— David Bayles

You can measure your worth by your dedication to your path,
not by your successes or failures.

— Elizabeth Gilbert

It's with colour that you put down this light of course, but above all,
you must feel this light, have it within yourself.

— Henri Matisse

You are an unfinished work in progress. One of the good things about life's challenges: you get to find out that you're capable of being far more than you ever thought possible.

— Karen Salmonsohn

Winter is an etching, spring a watercolor, summer an oil painting
and autumn a mosaic of them all.
— Stanley Horowitz

Love is the bridge between you and everything.

— Rumi

There is nothing on this earth more to be prized than true friendship.
—Thomas Aquinas

_____

_____

_____

_____

_____

_____

_____

_____

_____

_____

_____

If I stop and listen
I can hear a thousand heartbeats
of the birds and the bees
echoing around me
in the wind and the trees
If I stop and listen
I can hear a thousand songs
I can taste a thousand tears
of past and future stories
and seconds that stretch for years
can we just live our lives
lighter
Can we let our light shine
brighter
brave as we can be
to admit that we are free
as honest as we dare
to show the world, we care.

This is a time for fierce love, resilient love, a love that can move the mountains of outdated convention and weather the storm of turbulent change. A love that is unyielding in the face of fear and unconditional in the face of pain. A love that is relentlessly compassionate to ourselves and others as we navigate this monumental growth. Burn steady dear heart, burn bright and shine light into all the dark corners so that we can heal and arise strong together.